My Very First OXFORD Dictionary

My name is

'For Rose, Amy and Eleanor' — C.K.

OXFORD
UNIVERSITY PRESS

Great Clarendon Street, Oxford OX2 6DP

Oxford University Press is a department of the University of Oxford.
It furthers the University's objective of excellence in research, scholarship,
and education by publishing worldwide in

Oxford New York

Athens Auckland Bangkok Bogotá Buenos Aires Calcutta
Cape Town Chennai Dar es Salaam Delhi Florence Hong Kong Istanbul
Karachi Kuala Lumpur Madrid Melbourne Mexico City Mumbai
Nairobi Paris São Paulo Singapore Taipei Tokyo Toronto Warsaw

with associated companies in Berlin Ibadan

Oxford is a registered trade mark of Oxford University Press
in the UK and in certain other countries

British Library Cataloguing in Publication Data
Data available

ISBN 0-19-910503-0 (paperback)
ISBN 0-19-910502-2 (hardback)
ISBN 0-19-910562-6 (Big Book)
1–3–5–7–9–10–8–6–4–2

Typeset in Gill Sans Schoolbook
Printed in China

dog

You can keep a dog as a pet.

dress

A girl sometimes wears a dress.

doll

A doll is a toy person.

drink

You can drink milk.

door

You open a door to go into a room.

duck

A duck is a bird that likes water.

a b c **d** e f g h i j k l m n o p q r s t u v w x y z

Ee

eat

You need to eat food to live.

ear

You use your ears to hear.

egg

A bird lives inside an egg before it is born.

earth

You live on the planet Earth.

elbow

You bend your arm at your elbow.

electricity

You use electricity to get light and heat.

envelope

You put a letter in an envelope.

elephant

An elephant has a long nose called a trunk.

exercise

You need to exercise to keep fit.

empty

If something is empty it has nothing in it.

eye

You use your eyes to see.

a b c d **e** f g h i j k l m n o p q r s t u v w x y z

Ff

farm

A farm is where food is grown.

fairy

You can read about a fairy in stories.

feather

Birds have feathers instead of fur or hair.

fall

You come down quickly when you fall.

fish

A fish lives under water.

flower

A flower is part of a plant.

fox

A fox is a wild animal with a furry tail.

foot

Your foot is at the end of your leg.

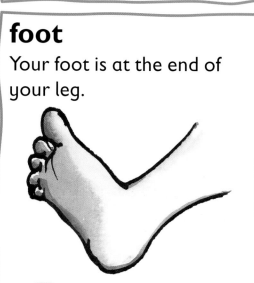

frog

A frog has wet skin and webbed feet.

fork

You use a fork to eat.

fruit

You can eat fruit. Apples and oranges are fruit.

a b c d e **f** g h i j k l m n o p q r s t u v w x y z

Gg

garden
You can grow flowers and vegetables in a garden.

game
You play a game.

gate
A gate is an outside door.

garage
A car is kept in a garage.

giant
A giant is a very big person.

giraffe

A giraffe has a long neck.

good

If something is good you like it.

glass

A window is made of glass.

grow

Things get bigger when they grow.

glue

You use glue to stick things together.

guitar

A guitar is an instrument with strings.

a b c d e f **g** h i j k l m n o p q r s t u v w x y z

Hh

head

Your eyes and ears are on your head.

hand

You hold things with your hand.

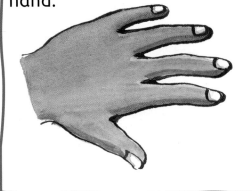

helicopter

A helicopter has blades that spin round on top.

hat

You wear a hat on your head.

hill

A hill is a piece of high land.

holiday

A holiday is when you do not go to school or work.

hot

If something is hot it can burn you.

horse

You can ride a horse.

house

You can live in a house.

hospital

You go to hospital if you are ill.

hungry

If you are hungry you want to eat.

Ii

information

You use information to find out about things.

ice

Freezing water turns to ice.

insect

An insect is a small animal with six legs.

ill

If you are ill you do not feel well.

instrument

You use an instrument to make music.

Jj

jug
You use a jug to pour a drink.

jam
You make jam from fruit and sugar.

STRAWBE
JAM

juggler
A juggler throws things up and catches them.

journey
You travel from place to place on a journey.

jump
You go up into the air when you jump.

a b c d e f g h i **j** k l m n o p q r s t u v w x y z

Kk

kettle

You use a kettle to boil water.

kangaroo

A kangaroo has big back legs and jumps.

key

You use a key to unlock a door.

keep

If you keep something you do not give it away.

kick

You kick a ball with your foot.

kind
You are being kind when you help other people.

kite
A kite flies in the air at the end of a long string.

king
Some countries are ruled by a king.

knee
Your knee is where your leg bends.

kitchen
You cook in a kitchen.

knife
You use a knife to cut things.

a b c d e f g h i j **k** l m n o p q r s t u v w x y z

Ll

leaf

A leaf grows on a plant.

ladybird

A ladybird is a small flying insect with spots.

leg

You use your legs to walk.

laugh

You laugh when something is funny.

letter

You use letters to write words.

library

Books are kept in a library.

little

If something is little it is not big.

like

If you like someone you think they are nice.

look

You use your eyes to look.

lion

A lion is a big wild cat.

loud

You can hear loud sounds easily.

a b c d e f g h i j k **l** m n o p q r s t u v w x y z

Mm

meat

We eat meat from animals.

make

You make something by putting things together.

metal

Something made of metal is hard.

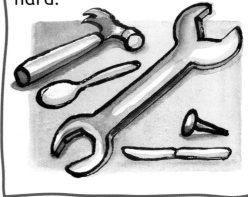

map

A map shows you how to get to places.

microwave

A microwave oven cooks food quickly.

milk

You can drink cow's milk.

moon

You often see the moon in the sky at night.

money

You use money to buy things.

mountain

A mountain is a high hill.

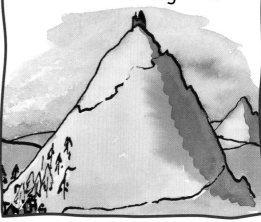

monkey

A monkey is furry and lives in trees.

mouth

You use your mouth to speak and eat.

a b c d e f g h i j k l **m** n o p q r s t u v w x y z

Nn

necklace

You wear a necklace around your neck.

name

Your name is what people call you.

nest

A bird lives in a nest.

neck

Your neck joins your head to your shoulders.

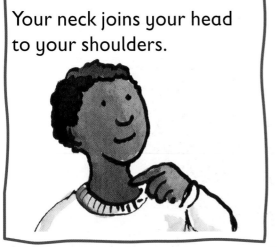

new

Something is new when you first get it.

nice

If something is nice you enjoy it.

nose

You use your nose to smell.

night

It is dark at night time.

number

You use numbers to count.

noise

A noise is a loud sound.

nurse

A nurse looks after you when you are ill.

a b c d e f g h i j k l m n o p q r s t u v w x y z

Oo

open
You can open a door.

octopus
An octopus has eight arms.

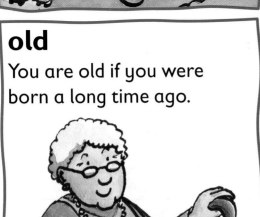

orange
An orange is a round fruit with thick peel.

old
You are old if you were born a long time ago.

owl
An owl is a bird who flies at night.

P p

park

You can play in a park.

page

A page is part of a book.

pencil

You use a pencil to write or draw.

paper

You write on paper.

piano

A piano is an instrument with black and white keys.

a b c d e f g h i j k l m n o **p** q r s t u v w x y z

pig
A pig is a fat farm animal.

play
You have fun when you play.

plant
A plant grows out of the ground.

pull
You can pull with your arms.

plate
You put food on a plate.

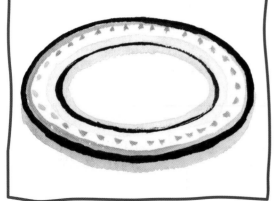

push
You push a wheelbarrow.

Q q

queue
You line up in a queue to wait for a bus.

queen
A queen is a woman who rules a country.

quick
You are quick when you move fast.

question
You ask a question to find out something.

quiet
You are quiet when you make very little noise.

a b c d e f g h i j k l m n o p q r s t u v w x y z

Rr

rainbow

Sun shines through rain to make a rainbow.

rabbit

A rabbit is a small animal with long ears.

read

You read books, cards and letters.

rain

The rain is water falling from the sky.

recorder

A recorder is an instrument that you blow.

rhinoceros

A rhinoceros has a horn on its nose.

robot

A robot is a machine that moves like a person.

river

A river is a large stream of water.

rocket

A rocket sends spacecraft into space.

road

Cars and buses travel on a road.

run

You move your legs quickly to run.

Ss

seed
A plant grows from a seed.

school
You go to school to learn.

sheep
You get wool from a sheep.

scissors
You use scissors to cut things.

shirt
A shirt has sleeves and a collar.

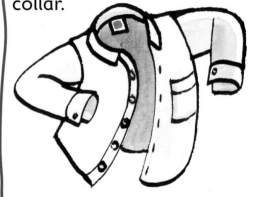

a b c d e f g h i j k l m n o p q r **s** t u v w x y z

shoe

You wear a shoe on your foot.

sock

You wear a sock on your foot.

shop

You buy things in a shop.

story

A story tells you about something that has happened.

snow

Snow falls when it is very cold.

sun

It is warm and bright in the sun.

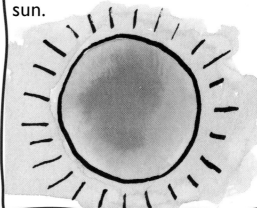

a b c d e f g h i j k l m n o p q r s **t** u v w x y z

Tt

teeth

You use your teeth to bite.

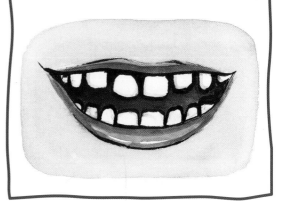

table

You sit at a table.

telephone

You use a telephone to speak to people.

teacher

A teacher helps you to learn.

television

You watch and listen to things on television.

towel

You use a towel to dry yourself.

train

A train goes on a track.

town

There are lots of buildings in a town.

tree

A tree is a tall plant with leaves.

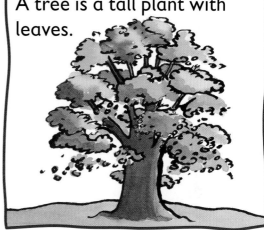

toy

You play with a toy.

trousers

You wear trousers on your legs.

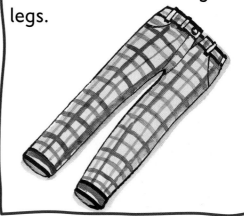

a b c d e f g h i j k l m n o p q r **s** **t** u v w x y z

Uu

uniform

The police and nurses wear a uniform.

ugly

If something is ugly it is not nice to look at.

upset

You are not happy when you are upset.

umbrella

You use an umbrella to keep dry when it rains.

use

You use tools to make things.

Vv

vegetable
A vegetable is a plant that you can eat.

van
A van can carry lots of things.

video
A video records sound and pictures from the television.

vase
You put flowers in a vase.

violin
You play a violin with a bow.

a b c d e f g h i j k l m n o p q r s t u **v** w x y z

Ww

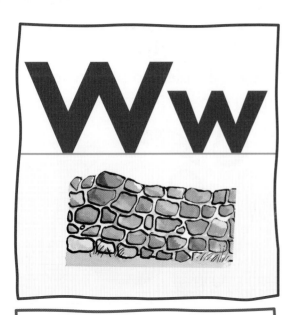

wind

The wind is air moving.

wall

A wall is made of brick or stone.

word

You use words when you speak or write.

water

Rivers and seas are made up of water.

write

You write words for other people to read.

X x

Y y

X-ray

An X-ray shows the inside of your body.

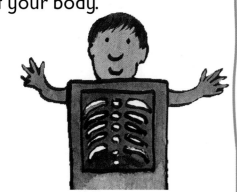

yacht

A yacht is a boat with sails.

xylophone

A xylophone is an instrument with wooden bars.

yawn

You yawn when you are tired.

a b c d e f g h i j k l m n o p q r s t u v w x y z

a b c d e f g h i j k l m n o p q r s t u v w x y z

year

There are twelve months in a year.

yogurt

You make yogurt from sour milk.

zebra

A zebra has black and white stripes.

young

You are young if you were born a short time ago.

zigzag

A zigzag line turns sharply.

zip

You do some coats up with a zip.

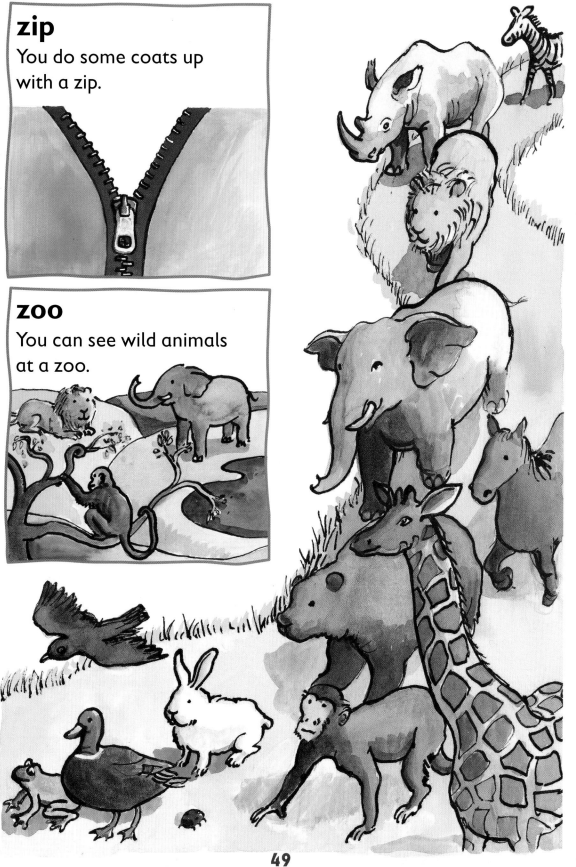

zoo

You can see wild animals at a zoo.

a b c d e f g h i j k l m n o p q r s t u v w x y z

Words we write a lot

a
about
after
again
all
am
an
and
another
are
as
at
away

back
ball
be
because
bed
been
big
boy
brother
but
by

call
called
came
can
can't
cat
children
come
could
cross

dad
day
did
dig
do
dog
don't
door
down

end
every
everyone

first
for
from

get
girl
go
going
good
got

had
half
has
have
he
help
her
here
him
his
home
house
how

I
if
in
is
it

jump
just

last
laugh
like
liked
little
live
lived
look
looked
lots
love

made
make
man
many
may
me
more
much
mum
must
my

name	said	under
new	saw	up
next	school	us
night	see	
no	seen	very
not	she	
now	should	want
	sister	was
of	sit	water
off	so	way
old	some	we
on		went
once	take	were
one	than	what
or	thank	when
our	that	where
out	the	who
over	their	why
	them	will
people	then	with
play	there	would
please	these	
pull	they	yes
pulled	this	you
push	three	your
put	time	
	to	
ran	too	
	took	
	tree	
	two	

Verbs (These are doing words)

add

carry

cry

catch

bounce

cut
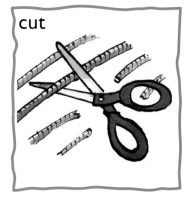

clap

buy

dance

climb

call

dig

cook

drink

grow

keep

eat

hear

kick

help

exercise

laugh

hop

fall

jump

like

More verbs

listen

look

make

open

paint

play

pull

push

read

run

see

sing

sit

sleep

talk

walk

smell

taste

wash

smile

throw

write

touch

take

use

yawn

Colours

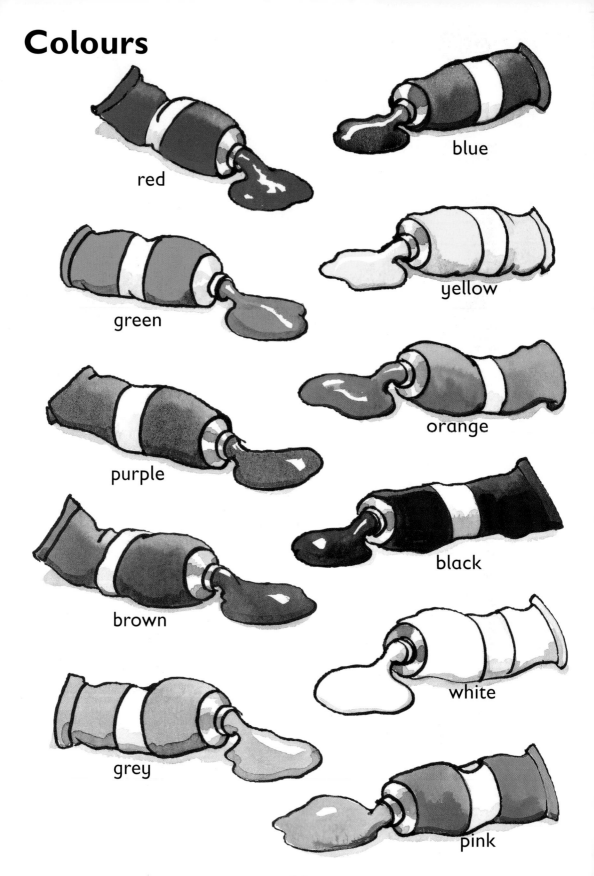

red

blue

green

yellow

purple

orange

brown

black

grey

white

pink

Shapes

square

triangle

circle

rectangle

Days of the week

Sunday

Monday

Saturday

Tuesday

Friday

Wednesday

Thursday

Months of the year

January

July

February

August

March

September

April

October

May

November

June

December

Numbers

zero	**0**	
one	1	🧦
two	**2**	🧦🧦
three	**3**	🧦🧦🧦
four	4	🧦🧦🧦🧦
five	**5**	🧦🧦🧦🧦🧦
six	**6**	🧦🧦🧦🧦🧦🧦
seven	**7**	🧦🧦🧦🧦🧦🧦🧦
eight	8	🧦🧦🧦🧦🧦🧦🧦🧦
nine	**9**	🧦🧦🧦🧦🧦🧦🧦🧦🧦

ten   **10**

eleven   **11**

twelve   **12**

thirteen   **13**

fourteen   **14**

fifteen   **15**

sixteen   **16**

seventeen   **17**

eighteen   **18**

nineteen   **19**

twenty   **20**

The alphabet

A a

B b

C c

D d

E e

F f

G g

H h

I i

J j

K k

L l

Mm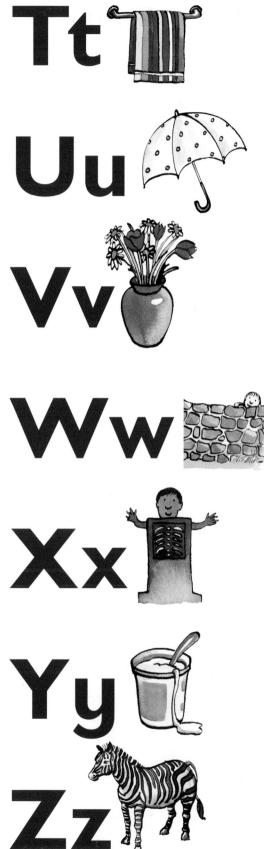

Tt

Nn

Uu

Oo

Vv

Pp

Ww

Qq

Xx

Rr

Yy

Ss

Zz